ON HOPE

JOSEF PIEPER

ON HOPE

TRANSLATED BY
SISTER MARY FRANCES McCARTHY, S.N.D.

IGNATIUS PRESS   SAN FRANCISCO

Title of the German original:
Über die Hoffnung
© ⁷1977 by Kösel-Verlag
GmbH & Co., München

Cover by Victoria Hoke Lane

© 1986 Ignatius Press, San Francisco
All rights reserved
ISBN 0-89870-067-1
Library of Congress Catalogue Number 85-82177
Printed in the United States of America

CONTENTS

Reflections on the concept *status viatoris*	9
Hope as a virtue	23
Anticipation of nonfulfillment (despair)	45
Anticipation of fulfillment (presumption)	63
The gift of fear	75
Author's remarks	89
Translator's note	93

"Although he should slay me,
I will trust in him" (Job 13:15).

Chapter One

REFLECTIONS ON THE CONCEPT
STATUS VIATORIS

Pastoral melodramatics have robbed the reference to man as a "pilgrim on this earth" and to his earthly life as a "pilgrimage" of its original significance and virility as well as its effectiveness. It no longer clearly mirrors the reality it is intended to convey. Its original meaning has been overgrown with a welter of extraneous aesthetic connotations; it has been all but buried under a veil of discordant secondary meanings, the false sentimentality of which actually destroys the joy that contemporary man—above all the younger generation and, perhaps, precisely the best of them—would have experienced in striving toward the reality that is ultimately reflected in the metaphor.

Nevertheless, this reality is part of the very foundation of being in the world for the Christian: the concept of the *status viatoris* is one of the basic concepts of every Christian rule of life.

To be a "viator" means "one on the way". The *status viatoris* is, then, the "condition or state of being on the way". Its proper antonym is *status comprehensoris*. One who has comprehended, encompassed, arrived, is no longer a *viator*, but a *comprehensor*. Theology has borrowed this word from one of Paul's epistles: "Brethren, I do not consider that I have laid hold [*comprehendisse*] of [the goal] already" (Phil 3:13). To be on the way, to be a *viator*, means to be making progress toward eternal happiness; to have encompassed this goal, to be a *comprehensor*, means to possess beatitude.[1] Beatitude is to be understood primarily as the fulfillment objectively appropriate to our nature, and only secondarily as the subjective response to this fulfillment. And this fulfillment is the Beatific Vision.

The concepts *status viatoris* and *status comprehensoris* designate the natural states of being of all creatures—above all, of man. Nearly every theological statement about men (or angels) refers more or less explicitly to one or the other of these concepts; and it is astonishing how many basic concepts of theology have a meaning in reference to the state of being on the way that is different from their meaning in reference to the state of total possession.

It would be difficult to conceive of another statement that penetrates as deeply into the innermost core of creaturely existence as does the statement that man finds himself, even until the moment of his death, in the *status viatoris*, in the state of being on the way.

Although it is almost literally as high as heaven above the enlightened despair of secular man, the

[1] III, 15, 10.

meaning this statement has acquired in popular piety—that the human soul comes, after the unrest of earthly life, into the peace of its heavenly home—is, nonetheless, but the easily remembered, figurative formulation of a metaphysical concept that is only partly comprehensible to the popular mind, and its clarification of which can lead the human spirit to the deepest knowledge of its own existence.

The state of being on the way is not to be understood in a primary and literal sense as a designation of place. It refers rather to the innermost structure of created nature. It is the inherent "not yet" of the finite being.

The "not yet" of the *status viatoris* includes both a negative and a positive element: the absence of fulfillment and the orientation toward fulfillment.

Fundamental to and constitutive of the negative side of the *status viatoris* is the proximity to nothingness that is the very nature of created things. The creature's relationship to nothingness has its roots in the primordial fact that whatever has been created has been created out of nothing. This is evident in the reverse side of human freedom, in the possibility of sinning; for sin is nothing other than a turning aside to nothingness. "In the natural course of events, the possibility of sinning cannot be taken from the creature endowed with intelligence; for by the very fact that it stems from nothingness, its power can revert to non-being."[2] Dissolution of the *status viatoris* and entrance into the *status comprehensoris* means that this power of the creature freely to turn toward nothingness is "linked" (*ligatur*[3]) to pure being by a grace-filled union. Freedom to sin is turned into the greater freedom of not being able to sin.[4]

The positive side of the concept of being on the way, the creature's natural orientation toward fulfillment, is revealed, above all, in man's ability to establish, by his own effort, a kind of justifiable "claim" to the happy outcome of his pilgrimage. This ability is none other than the possibility of meritorious action, which has the character of genuine "progress". (This does not alter the fact that "meritorious" action presumes the pre-existence of something that cannot be "merited".) The *status comprehensoris* fulfills the "claim" of these "merits"; in consequence, the possibility of meritorious action ceases to exist just as does the freedom to sin. In the transition from the state of being on the way to that of *status comprehensoris*, then, the *status viatoris* is dissolved in both its negative and its positive aspects: the possibility of turn-

[2] 2, d. 23, 1.
[3] 2, d. 23, 1.
[4] I, 62, 8 ad 3.

ing toward nothingness is abolished by union; the claim to and the orientation toward fulfillment are abolished by the reality of fulfillment.

The *status viatoris* comes to an end at the moment when uncertainty comes to border on certainty. This moment puts its seal not only on fulfillment, but also on nonfulfillment. Even the decision in favor of nothingness becomes definitive at this time. The state of being on the way is dissolved in either case; even "Satan immediately lost the *status viatoris* by his sin."[5]

Eternal damnation is the irrevocable fixing of the will on nothingness, just as the *status comprehensoris* is the *confirmatio in bono*, the "fastening" of the will on the highest being. In damnation, the positive side of the *status viatoris*, the orientation toward fulfillment, is definitively cut off and destroyed; thus isolated, the negative side becomes an absolute value. The inner "not yet" that once characterized the creature's nature is changed into a characteristic inner "not".

The "way" of man leads to death. Since man, by his sin, came under the law of death at the beginning of his history, his life has become an incipient

[5] Mal., 16, 5.

death.⁶ The "way" of man leads to death as its end, but not as its meaning. The meaning of the *status viatoris* is the *status comprehensoris*.

For man, then, the *status viatoris* lasts as long as he lives in the body; the *status viatoris* ends when he ceases to live in the body. For that reason, man's "way" is "temporality". Time, in fact, exists only in reference to the transitoriness of man. The union of his spirit with his body is the foundation of his union with time; spirit itself, including man's spirit, is "above time".⁷ In death, since man then leaves the *status viatoris*, he also steps out of time. This does not mean, however, that he enters into the realm of God's own eternity.⁸

Present-day existential philosophy, which regards human existence exclusively in its temporality as a "being in time", is right to the extent that it opposes an idealistic doctrine of man in which the *status viatoris* seems transformed, against its nature, into a permanent likeness to God. But to the extent that this existential philosophy conceives of man's existence as essentially and "in the foundation of its being temporal" (Heidegger), it too fails to comprehend the true nature of its subject. Anyone, in other words, who seeks to understand

⁶ De pec., I, 16.
⁷ I, II, 53, 3 ad 3.
⁸ I, 10, 5.

temporality without restriction as the necessary mark of human existence will find hidden from him not only the "life beyond" time, but also the very meaning of life *in* time. Idealism fails to recognize the nature of human existence because it "omits" the *status viatoris*; existentialism fails to recognize the true nature of human existence because it denies the "pilgrimage" character of the *status viatoris*, its orientation toward fulfillment beyond time, and hence, in principle, the *status viatoris* itself.

Even the angels, whether blessed or fallen, were once, in the strict sense, *viatores*, "on the way". But their "way" was not "temporality" (which, again, does not mean they shared in the eternity of God). For the angel, the *status viatoris* was a single instant—"instant", too, refers to time, but we are unable to think in anything but a temporal mode—an instant in which the angel was able to make an intellectual decision for or against God. From the first moment of his existence, the angel stood "at the end of his pilgrimage";[9] the duration of a single unpropitious act of decision separated him from his goal. For the angel, this act put an end to the *status viatoris*.

Saint Thomas says that God decided on a

[9] Quol., 9, 8 ad 2.

"longer way" for men than for angels because, in the graduated order of their natures, man is more distant from God, *magis a Deo distans*.[10]

The concept of the *status viatoris* designates, in a special sense, the inner structure of man's creatureliness.

The creatureliness of man reveals itself above all in the deep differentiation of being with regard to God that expresses the fundamental principle of the "analogy of being". This differentiation of being consists primarily in the fact that God is he who is absolute being, in the fullness of whose being essence and existence are one; whereas man is not ipso facto his own essence; his essence is "in the process of becoming". This becoming-ness of the creature is especially evident in the concept of the *status viatoris*; in the "not yet" of man's being on the way, the whole span of the creature's "becoming-ness" (Przywara) is revealed, as in a concave mirror, between the shores of being and nothingness.

To be a creature means "to be imprisoned in nothingness" (Heidegger); even more, it means being grounded in absolute being and having an existential orientation toward being, toward one's own

[10] 2, d. 7, 1, 2; cf. 2, d. 23, 1, 2 ad 2; I, 62, 5 ad 1.

being and, at the same time, toward the divine being.[11] And this is as it should be: "Just as they have their source in nothingness, so created beings could sink back into nothingness if that were pleasing to God";[12] but "He created all things that they might be" (Wis 1:14). Among the numerous objections that Saint Thomas raises against his theses in the *Quaestiones Disputatae*, there is one that might stand word for word in the tomes of nihilistic existential philosophy today: *proprius motus naturae ex nihilo existentis est ut in nihilum tendat*: the proper movement of a being that stems from nothingness is to tend toward nothingness.[13] To this objection the "universal teacher" of the Church responds as follows: the orientation toward nothingness is not the proper movement of natural being, which is always directed toward a good (but "good" means "existence"); the orientation toward nothingness comes into existence precisely through the rejection of this proper movement.[14] Despite every possibility of falling into nothingness, the proper orientation of the "way" is toward being—to such an extent that, to be possible, even the decision in favor of nothingness

[11] Pot., 5, 4.
[12] Pot., 5, 4 ad 10.
[13] Pot., 5, 1, obj. 16.
[14] Pot., 5, 1 ad 16.

would have to wear the mask of a decision for being.

The whole span of creaturely existence between being and nothingness can never be understood, then, as though the relationship to nothingness were simply to be assigned equal rank with the relationship to being—or were even to be ranked before or above it. The "way" of *homo viator*, of man "on the way", is not a directionless back-and-forth between being and nothingness; it leads toward being and away from nothingness; it leads to realization, not to annihilation, although this realization is "not yet" fulfilled and the fall into nothingness is "not yet" impossible.

For the individual who experiences, in the *status viatoris*, his essential creatureliness, the "not-yet-existing-being" of his own existence, there is only *one* appropriate answer to such an experience. This answer must not be despair—for the meaning of the creature's existence is not nothingness but being, that is, fulfillment. Nor must the answer be the comfortable certainty of possession—for the "becoming-ness" of the creature still borders dangerously on nothingness. Both—despair and the certainty of possession—are in conflict with the truth of reality. The only answer that corresponds to man's actual existential situation is hope.

The virtue of hope is preeminently the virtue of the *status viatoris*; it is the proper virtue of the "not yet".

In the virtue of hope more than in any other, man understands and affirms that he is a creature, that he has been created by God.

Chapter Two

HOPE AS A VIRTUE

It would never occur to a philosopher, unless he were also a Christian theologian, to describe hope as a virtue. For hope is either a theological virtue or not a virtue at all. It becomes a virtue by becoming a theological virtue.[1]

Virtue is not the tame "respectability" and "uprightness" of the philistine, but the enhancement of the human person in a way befitting his nature. Virtue is the *ultimum potentiae*,[2] the most a man can be. It is the realization of man's potentiality for being. Virtue is the perfecting of man for an activity by which he achieves his beatitude.[3] Virtue means the steadfastness of man's orientation toward the realization of his nature, that is, toward good.

Theological virtue is an ennobling of man's nature that entirely surpasses what he "can be" of himself. Theological virtue is the steadfast orientation toward a fulfillment and a beatitude that are not "owed" to natural man. Theological virtue is the utmost degree of a supernatural potentiality for being. This supernatural potentiality for being is grounded in a real, grace-filled participation in the divine nature, which comes to man through Christ (2 Pet 1:4).

[1] I, II, 62, 3 ad 2.
[2] Virt. card., 3.
[3] I, II, 62, 1.

First, then, that steadfast orientation toward fulfillment that we call "theological" virtue has its source in a truly divine substance in man, in grace.[4] Secondly, it is aimed directly at supernatural happiness in God who is known in a supernatural manner. Finally, it is only through divine revelation that the existence, origin and object of this theological virtue are known to us.

When we say, then, that hope is a virtue only when it is a theological virtue, we mean that hope is a steadfast turning toward the true fulfillment of man's nature, that is, toward good, only when it has its source in the reality of grace in man and is directed toward supernatural happiness in God.

Justice, for instance, is already a true virtue, a clear tending toward good, even outside the supernatural order. When justice ceases to be directed toward good, it ceases to be justice. Hope, on the other hand, can also be directed—even in the natural sphere—toward what is objectively bad and yet remain real hope. Natural hope lacks the distinctive quality of virtue: *quod ita sit principium actus boni, quod nullo modo mali*—that it is so ordered to good that it cannot possibly turn toward evil.[5]

---

[4] I, II, 62, 1.
[5] Virt. comm., 2.

Obviously, hope experiences this firmness of orientation toward good above all as a God-given turning to God, that is, as a theological virtue.

Hope, like love, is one of the very simple, primordial dispositions of the living person. In hope, man reaches "with restless heart", with confidence and patient expectation, toward the *bonum arduum futurum*, toward the arduous "not yet" of fulfillment, whether natural or supernatural.

As we have said above, the patient expectation of the emotional-intellectual hope of natural man does not include, of itself, that certainty of being ordered toward true good that is the definitive mark of true virtue. But this natural expectation—as adaptable matter, as receptive *materia*—tends by its very nature to be stamped with the formative standard of virtue so that it may itself, by reason of this standard, gain a share in the orientation toward good.

As *materia*, the disposition of sensuous-intellectual hope that aspires to the "not yet" of man's natural fulfillment is ordered to two virtues in particular: magnanimity (*magnanimitas*) and humility.[6]

---

[6] II, II, 161, 1.

The proper impulse of natural hope, as such, is toward the virtue of magnanimity. Humility is the protective barrier and restraining wall of this impulse.

Magnanimity, a much-forgotten virtue, is the aspiration of the spirit to great things, *extensio animi ad magna*.[7] A person is magnanimous if he has the courage to seek what is great and becomes worthy of it. This virtue has its roots in a firm confidence in the highest possibilities of that human nature that God did "marvelously ennoble and has still more marvelously renewed" (Roman Missal).[8] Thus magnanimity incorporates into itself the aspiration of natural hope and stamps it according to the truth of man's own nature. Magnanimity, as both Thomas and Aristotle tell us, is "the jewel of all the virtues",[9] since it always—and particularly in ethical matters—decides in favor of what is, at any given moment, the greater possibility of the human potentiality for being. It is good to think that, in this way, every virtue is borne along on a current that receives and guards the courageous unrest of our natural hope.

Humility, which is only apparently the opposite of magnanimity,[10] is not, in any sense, a forgotten

[7] II, II, 129, 1.
[8] II, II, 129, 3 ad 4.
[9] II, II, 129, 4 ad 3.
[10] II, II, 129, 3 ad 4.

virtue, but it is one that is often misinterpreted and misunderstood. To anticipate the grossest misunderstanding, humility is not only not itself an external attitude; it is also not bound to any external attitude. Humility rests on an interior decision of the will.[11] Furthermore, humility is not primarily an attitude that pertains to the relationship of man to man: it is the attitude of man before the face of God.[12] Humility is the knowledge and acceptance of the inexpressible distance between Creator and creature. It is, in a very precise sense, as Gertrud von le Fort once said, "man's true and proper worth before God". Man's worth, as that of a being possessed of a soul, consists solely in this: that, by his own free decision, he knows and acts in accordance with the reality of his nature—that is, in truth.

But let us return to our subject: humility and natural hope. It is the function of humility to be the negative measure of instinctive-natural hope. Magnanimity directs this hope to its true possibilities; humility, with its gaze fixed on the infinite distance between man and God, reveals the limitations of these possibilities and preserves them from sham realization and for true realization.

[11] II, II, 161, 1 ad 2.
[12] II, II, 161, 1 ad 5.

The proper ordering of natural hope is born, then, from the interaction of magnanimity and humility.

This explains the fact that these two natural virtues, magnanimity and humility, are the most essential prerequisites for the preservation and unfolding of supernatural hope—insofar as this depends on man. Together they represent the most complete preparedness of the natural man, whose existence is "postulated" by grace.

On the other hand, the culpable loss of supernatural hope has its roots in two principal sources: lack of magnanimity and lack of humility. This remains to be discussed.

The supernatural life in man has three main currents: the reality of God, which surpasses all natural knowledge "not only of men, but also of angels",[13] manifests itself to faith. Love affirms—also in its own right—the Highest Good, which has become visible beneath the veil of faith. Hope is the confidently patient expectation of eternal beatitude in a contemplative and comprehensive sharing of the triune life of God; hope expects from God's hand the eternal life that is God himself: *sperat Deum a Deo*.[14]

[13] Contra Graecos, caput II.
[14] Cajetan, Commentary on II, II, 17, 5; Nr. 7.

HOPE AS A VIRTUE

The existential relationship of these three—faith, hope, love—can be expressed in three sentences. First: faith, hope and love have all three been implanted in human nature as natural inclinations (*habitus*) conjointly with the reality of grace, the one source of all supernatural life. Second: in the orderly sequence of the active development of these supernatural inclinations, faith takes precedence over both hope and love; hope takes precedence over love;[15] conversely, in the culpable disorder of their dissolution, love is lost first, then hope, and, last of all, faith.[16] Third: in the order of perfection, love holds first place, with faith last, and hope between them.[17]

It remains, now, to shed further light on the relationship between hope and love by means of a distinction—a distinction, namely, between the perfect love of friendship (*amor amicitiae*) and the imperfect love of "concupiscence" (*amor concupiscentiae*), that is, between a love that loves the beloved for his sake and one that loves him for its own sake.

The virtue of hope is associated primarily with that *im*perfect love of God that desires God, the Highest Good, only for its own sake. Indeed, it

[15] I, II, 62, 4.
[16] De spe, 3 ad 11.
[17] Virt. card., 3.

belongs to the concept and nature of hope that one can hope only for oneself (and for him whom one loves, for the "other self").[18] Nevertheless, this imperfect love of hope—Francis de Sales calls it *amour d'espérance*—is the not-to-be-undervalued precursor of the perfect love of friendship (*caritas*) by which God is affirmed for his own sake. And the perfect love of God, which is the theological virtue of love and, at the same time, the mother and root of all Christian virtues, flows back again on hope to mold and enhance it.[19]

"Thus the theological virtues flow back upon themselves in a sacred circle: one who is led to love by hope has thereafter a more perfect hope, just as he also believes now more strongly than before."[20]

The assumption that the existence of a "concupiscent" love of God that is referred by hope to oneself, and hence that hope itself, is no more than an "interested" and "mercenary" love unworthy of the truly perfect Christian (as though man could possibly be "disinterested" in the fulfillment of his own nature in God—for what else is "heaven" all about?) belongs, it would seem, to those inevitable

[18] De spe, 3.
[19] I, II, 62, 4.
[20] De spe, 3 ad 1.

temptations to pride by which even the strongest souls are endangered. The Council of Trent has spoken authoritatively on this subject: "If anyone says that the faithful ought not to expect and hope for eternal happiness from God for the sake of his mercy and the merits of Jesus Christ . . . , let him be anathema."[21] Two hundred years earlier, Saint Bonaventure had written in his *Commentary on the Sentences of Peter Lombard*: "There are many who look for beatitude, but worry little about themselves and much about God."[22]

It is very difficult to keep in mind the fundamentally incomprehensible fact that hope, as a virtue, is something wholly supernatural. Certainly, man's innate capability plays a role in the gaining of that for which he hopes, that is, of eternal happiness. "But the very habit of hope [*ipse habitus spei*], by virtue of which one expects happiness, stems not from merit, but solely from grace."[23] In his excellent study of the theological virtues, the holy Paschasius Radbert, a great Frankish theologian of the Carolingian period, expressed this thought in the following words: "Christ is held by the hand of hope. We hold him and are held. But it

[21] Council of Trent, sessio VI, cap. 16, can. 26, p. 799.
[22] St. Bonaventure, 3, d. 26, 1, 1 ad 5.
[23] II, II, 17, 1 ad 2.

is a greater good that we are held by Christ than that we hold him. For we can hold him only so long as we are held by him."[24]

(It follows, incidentally, from the supernatural character of hope that what we must say and write about this "infused" virtue differs from what we would say and write about courage, for instance, or justice. A discussion about hope can seek to achieve only indirectly what can rightly be expected from a presentation of the "acquired", and therefore "acquirable", virtues—namely, that it be, at the same time, an incentive to the virtue in question.)

The embodiment, at once symbolic and truly fundamental, of the supernatural life in man is the man Christ, "in whom dwells the fullness of the Godhead". He is also the embodiment of our hope: "Christ in you, your hope of glory!" (Col 1:27). (How does it happen that we are so prone to understand Holy Scripture in a vague approximation rather than in the precise meaning of its passages? It is due in part, perhaps, to a decline in the proper dogmatic interpretation of Scripture.)

Christ is the actual foundation of hope. In a striking sentence, the letter to the Hebrews speaks of the hope we have "as a sure and firm anchor of the soul, reaching even behind the veil, where our

[24] De fide, spe et charitate, liber II, caput I.

forerunner Jesus has entered for us" (6:19). Thomas Aquinas comments: "Christ has entered for us into the inner sanctuary of the tent and has there made firm [*fixit*] our hope."[25]

Christ is, at the same time, the actual fulfillment of our hope. This fact is expressed with singular clarity in the passage in which Saint Augustine undertakes to interpret the scriptural text *spe salvi facti sumus*: "In hope were we saved" (Rom 8:24): "But Paul did not say, 'we shall be saved', but 'we have already been saved'; yet not in fact [*re*], but in hope; he says, 'in hope were we saved'." "This hope we have in Christ, for in him is fulfilled all that we hope for by his promise."[26] "As yet we do not see that for which we hope. But we are the body of that Head in whom that for which we hope is brought to fulfillment."[27]

This inherent linking of our hope to Christ is so crucial that one who is not in Christ has no hope (1 Thes 4:13).

The "Compendium of Theology", of which Saint Thomas had completed only about a third before his death, was intended to present the whole doctrine of salvation in three parts named after the three theological virtues. The second, largely un-

[25] Hebr., caput VI, lectio IV, p. 637.
[26] Contra Faustum, liber undecimus, caput VII, col. 251, PL 42.
[27] Sermo 157, 3, col. 860, PL 38.

finished part, which contains only a few chapters under the title "On Hope", was to have been an explanation of the Our Father. "Just as our Savior initiated and perfected our faith, so it was salutary that he should lead us to living hope by teaching us the prayer by which our hope is especially directed to God."[28]

Prayer and hope are naturally ordered to each other. Prayer is the expression and proclamation of hope; it is *interpretativa spei*;[29] hope itself speaks through it.

And all the prayers of the Church, "bolder [in their hope] than all the great thoughts of the philosophers", have the uniform conclusion: *per Christum Dominum nostrum*—through Christ, our Lord. This fact links the present discussion with those that have preceded it.

It will, perhaps, not be superfluous to state here that the three preceding sections present the central message of this book. They contain the core of the theological doctrine of hope. This core is the statement that hope, as the lasting elevation of man's being, cannot exist except from, through and in Christ.

As Bonaventure emphasized in his *Commentary on the Sentences of Peter Lombard*, the nature of the

[28] Comp., pars II, caput III.
[29] II, II, 17, 4.

HOPE AS A VIRTUE

certainty that appertains to hope is "hard to define".[30]

On the one hand, hope partakes of the unconditional certitude of faith,[31] on which it depends: hope is grounded above all in the divine mercy and omnipotence, "through which even one who does not possess grace can yet become a partaker of it in order thus to achieve everlasting life; everyone who has faith has also this certitude about the omnipotence and mercy of God."[32] Hope's unfailing certitude is based on this fact, that is, on the genuinely grace-filled nature of supernatural hope.

It is not certain, however, that man, of himself, will be able to "persevere in hope". As long as he is in the *status viatoris*, man, even the "perfect Christian", can, by turning aside to nothingness, use his free will to destroy the supernatural life that is in him and with it the hope of eternal life that is rooted therein. "It is not the certainty of hope that is thus denied",[33] but only the possibility of a subjective certainty of salvation.

Although all must place the firmest hope in God's help, no one must promise himself anything with absolute certainty. For God does, of course, perfect the good work he has begun by causing the

---

[30] St. Bonaventure, 3, d. 26, 1, 5.
[31] II, II, 18, 4.
[32] II, II, 18, 4 ad 2.
[33] II, II, 18, 4 ad 3.

will and the accomplishment if only they do not withdraw themselves from his grace. Yet those who believe themselves to stand should take care lest they fall and should work out their salvation in fear and trembling. . . . That is, they must fear, knowing that they have been born again unto the hope of glory, but not yet unto glory.[34]

However magnanimous he may be, natural man can never hope for the eternal life of the Beatific Vision of God without falling into pride (and thus ceasing to be magnanimous). Yet this supernatural fulfillment of man's nature, toward which the theological virtue of hope is directed, is, all unnoticed, the object of all natural hope. All our natural hopes tend toward fulfillments that are like vague mirrorings and foreshadowings of, like unconscious preparations for, eternal life.

In a certain sense, the virtue of hope brings order and direction in its wake even for man's natural hope, which is bound thereby to its proper and final "not yet": "in our orientation toward eternal life we hope to receive help from God not only for spiritual, but also for corporal deeds."[35] On the clear basis of this sentence from Saint Thomas Aquinas (in which he plainly says that it is permit-

[34] Council of Trent, sessio VI, cap. 13, p. 796.
[35] De spe, 1.

ted us to surround even the natural goods of life with supernatural hope, that is, with a hope directly infused by God), there become manifest—as faint foreshadowings, yet clearly visible to the devout eye—some of the basic structures on which the supernatural realm is built.

The ease with which an age living in the certainty of faith could combine natural with supernatural hope is almost incomprehensible to us today. It is very difficult for us to understand how unabashedly Dante, for instance, in the twenty-fifth canto of the *Paradiso* (Dante, in a dialogue with James, the Apostle of Hope, the "Baron" of heaven, unfolds in this canto of the *Divine Comedy* a whole theology of supernatural hope)—how unabashedly, I repeat, Dante, carried up to the "heavenly sphere of the fixed stars", gives free expression even to his earthly hope of returning to Florence in glory. ("If it should chance that e'er the sacred song / To which both Heaven and Earth have set their hand, / . . . Should touch the cruel hearts by which I'm banned / From my fair fold where as a lamb I lay, / . . . With altered voice, with altered fleece today / I shall return, a poet, at my font / Of baptism to take the crown of bay.")[36]

Supernatural hope, then, which embraces not only

[36] Paradise, canto 25, 1–9.

the firm expectation itself, but also the living source of this expectation, is able to rejuvenate and give new vigor even to natural hope. "Rejuvenate" is precisely the right word here. Youth and hope are ordered to one another in manifold ways. They belong together in the natural as well as in the supernatural sphere. The figure of youth is the eternal symbol of hope, just as it is the symbol of magnanimity.

Natural hope blossoms with the strength of youth and withers when youth withers. "Youth is a cause of hope. For youth, the future is long and the past is short."[37] On the other hand, it is above all when life grows short that hope grows weary; the "not yet" is turned into the has-been, and old age turns, not to the "not yet", but to memories of what is "no more".

For supernatural hope, the opposite is true: not only is it not bound to natural youth; it is actually rooted in a much more substantial youthfulness. It bestows on mankind a "not yet" that is entirely superior to and distinct from the failing strength of man's natural hope. Hence it gives man such a "long" future that the past seems "short" however long and rich his life. The theological virtue of hope is the power to wait patiently for a "not yet" that is the more immeasurably distant from us the more closely we approach it.

[37] I, II, 40, 6.

HOPE AS A VIRTUE

The supernatural vitality of hope overflows, moreover, and sheds its light also upon the rejuvenated powers of natural hope. The lives of countless saints attest to this truly astonishing fact. It seems surprising, however, how seldom the enchanting youthfulness of our great saints is noticed; especially of those saints who were active in the world as builders and founders. There is hardly anything comparable to just this youthfulness of the saint that testifies so challengingly to the fact that is surely most relevant for contemporary man: that, in the most literal sense of these words, nothing more eminently preserves and founds "eternal youth" than the theological virtue of hope. It alone can bestow on man the certain possession of that aspiration that is at once relaxed and disciplined, that adaptability and readiness, that strong-hearted freshness, that resilient joy, that steady preseverance in trust that so distinguish the young and make them lovable.

We must not regard this as a fatal concession to the *Zeitgeist*. As Saint Augustine so aptly says: "God is younger than all else."[38]

The gift of youth that supernatural hope bestows on man leaves its mark on human nature at a much deeper level than does natural youth. Despite its very visible effect in the natural sphere, the Chris-

[38] De genesi, liber VIII, caput 26, 48, col. 392, PL 34.

tian's supernaturally grounded youthfulness lives from a root that penetrates into an area of human nature that the powers of natural hope are unable to reach. This is so because the supernatural youthfulness emanates from participation in the life of God, who is closer and more intimate to us than we are to ourselves.

For this reason, the youthfulness of the individual who longs for eternal life is fundamentally imperishable. It cannot be touched by aging or disappointment; it proves itself above all in the face of the withering of natural youth and in temptations to despair. Saint Paul says, ". . . Even though our outer man is decaying, yet our inner man is being renewed day by day" (2 Cor 4:16). But there are no other words in Holy Scripture or in human speech as a whole that let resound as triumphantly the youthfulness of one who remains firm in hope against all destruction and through a veil of tears as do those of the patient Job: "Although he should slay me, I will trust in him . . ." (13:15).

This whole book about hope revolves around this sentence because I believe it is vitally important for an age from whose despair there seems to issue a forced and superficial cult of youthfulness to have a glimpse of the highest pinnacle to which the hope-filled youthfulness of those who entrust themselves to God can soar. Job's words cut the foundation, moreover, from under a misapprehension that can, in fact, be critical in a catastrophic age, namely, the mistaken assumption that the substance of natural hope can be encompassed by supernatural hope even from below (instead of from above); in other words, that the fulfillment of supernatural hope must occur through the fulfillment of natural hope. It might be well, at a time when temptations to despair abound, for a Christianity that labors hard to hold high the banner of hope in eternal life to help its "younger generation" to read and, above all, to understand Job's words at an early age.

Nonetheless, this chapter will conclude with the verses that occur at the end of the fortieth chapter, the famous chapter that contains the message of salvation, of the Book of Isaiah, the book of the hope and consolation of Israel—the verses that begin with the Advent *Consolamini*: "Be comforted, be comforted, my people" (Is 40:1). These verses—the German mystics would call them a *jubilus*—read as follows: "But they that hope in the Lord shall renew their strength; they shall take wings as eagles; they shall run and not be weary; they shall walk and not faint" (Is 40:31).

Chapter Three

ANTICIPATION OF NONFULFILLMENT (DESPAIR)

THERE ARE TWO KINDS of hopelessness. One is despair; the other, *praesumptio*.[1] *Praesumptio* is a perverse anticipation of the fulfillment of hope. Despair is also an anticipation—a perverse anticipation of the nonfulfillment of hope: "to despair is to descend into hell".[2]

By describing both despair and presumption as "anticipation", we disclose the fact that both of them destroy the pilgrim character of human existence in the *status viatoris*. For they are both opposed to man's true becoming. Against all reality, they transform the "not yet" of hope into either the "not" or the "already" of fulfillment. In despair as in presumption, that which is genuinely human—which alone is able to preserve the easy flow of hope—is paralyzed and frozen. Both

[1] Pieper takes exception here to the usual German translation of Latin *praesumptio* as *Vermessenheit* [overconfidence], preferring instead the linguistically and semantically more accurate translation *Vorwegnahme* [anticipation]. As a cognate of the Latin *praesumptio*, English "presumption" is, of course, etymologically close to the Latin original. Semantically, on the other hand, it has acquired, in everyday speech, much of the meaning associated with German *Vermessenheit*. I have, nevertheless, retained it in translation because it is the term most generally used in this context in theological writings in English [Tr.].

[2] Isidore, liber II, caput XIV, 2, col. 617, PL 83. Cited in II, II, 20, 3.

forms of hopelessness are, in the last analysis, unnatural and deadly. "There are two things that kill the soul," Saint Augustine tells us, "despair and false hope".[3] And Ambrose says, "He seems not to be human at all who does not hope in God."[4]

Today when we speak of despair we are usually referring to a psychological state into which an individual "falls" almost against his will. As it is here used, however, the term describes a decision of the will. Not a mood, but an act of the intellect. Hence not something into which one falls, but something one posits.

The despair of which we are speaking is a sin. A sin, moreover, that bears the mark of special gravity and of an intensity of evil.

Hope says: It will turn out well; or more accurately and characteristically: It will turn out well for mankind; or even more characteristically: It will turn out well for us, for me myself. To these characteristic degrees of hope there correspond the degrees of despair. The most characteristic form of despair says: It will turn out badly for us and for me myself.

It is essential for both hope and despair,

[3] Sermo 87, 8, col. 535, PL 38.
[4] De Isaac, caput I, 1, col. 527, PL 14.

ANTICIPATION OF NONFULFILLMENT

moreover, that these sentences not be understood in a merely "theoretical" sense. Both he who hopes and he who despairs choose these attitudes with their will and let them determine their conduct.

Both hope and despair are capable of varying degrees of depth. All manner of doubt can exist, as it were, closer to the surface above a hope that has its roots in the most interior depths of the soul. But these doubts do not touch the hope that is so deeply rooted; they have no ultimate significance. Similarly, an individual in the last stages of despair can, by reason of the natural and cultural forces in the penultimate regions of his soul, appear to others and even to himself to be an "optimist". He has only to seal off the innermost chamber of his despair so radically that no cry of pain can escape to the outer world (and there are many indications that man in the modern world has become a true virtuoso in this respect).

The deepest and most authentic depth of hope was opened up to mankind by the original event of the redemption. Through this event, too, the possibility of despair was increased by one more abyss of darkness. Natural man can never say as triumphantly as can the Christian: It will turn out well for me in the end. Nor can the hope of natural man look forward to an "end" like that of the Christian. But neither can a heathen be tempted to the same depths of despair as the Christian—and, indeed, as the greatest Christians and the saints. For the same flash of light that reveals to the creature the supernatural reality of grace lights up also the abyss of his guilt and his distance from God.

It makes a great difference, then, whether it is a Christian or a heathen who says: It will turn out badly for mankind, for us, for me myself.

The Christian who despairs about eternal life not only destroys the pilgrim character of his natural existence, but also denies the actual "way" to eternal happiness and fulfillment: Christ himself, who appeared in human form. "Despair has no foot on which to walk the way that is Christ", says Saint Paschasius Radbert.[5] (How little the primitive etymology on which this formulation of the truth is based—*spes–hope* is linked to *pes–foot*—is able to conceal or detract from its impressiveness!) For the Christian, despair is a decision against Christ. It is a denial of the redemption.

In despair, the nature of sin per se becomes es-

[5] *De fide, spe et charitate*, liber II, caput IV, 1.

pecially clear, namely, that it is in conflict with reality. Despair is a denial of the way of fulfillment—and this before the very eyes of him who is preeminently "the way" to eternal life.

It is not by chance, I think, that Thomas Aquinas, at the very beginning of the article entitled "Is Despair a Sin?", explicitly designates precisely this characteristic of sin (viz., that it contradicts reality) as the foundation of his argument: "Every movement of the will that is in conformity with true insight is good in itself, but every movement of the will that is the result of a false judgment is evil in itself and is a sin."[6] Elsewhere he says, "If sin could truly not be forgiven, then it would not be a sin to doubt the forgiveness of sin."[7]

Despair is the state of being which is proper to the damned. And the despair of one in the *status viatoris* is, as we have said, a kind of anticipation of damnation.

The pain of despair lies in the fact that it denies the way to fulfillment, which the nature of him who despairs does not cease to desire. Like hope, despair presumes the existence of a desire: "That

[6] II, II, 20, 1.
[7] Mal., 3, 15.

for which we have no desire can neither be the object of our hope nor of our despair".[8]

Despair is self-contradictory, self-divisive.[9] In despair man actually denies his own desire, which is as indestructible as himself.

Objectively speaking, despair is not the most serious sin. But it is the most dangerous of all.[10] It threatens man's moral existence, for man's self-realization is linked to hope. "It is not so much sin as despair that casts us into hell", says Saint John Chrysostom in his commentary on the Gospel of Saint Matthew.[11]

Since Peter Lombard composed his *Sentences*, the Church's theology has counted despair among the sins against the Holy Spirit. Despair moves thus into the vicinity of that dark mystery expressed by the Lord: ". . . Whoever speaks against the Holy Spirit, it will not be forgiven him, either in this world or in the world to come" (Mt 12:32). I say deliberately no more than that despair moves "into the vicinity" of this mystery. For Saint Thomas refers this word of the Lord solely to a

[8] I, II, 40, 4 ad 3.

[9] In a play on the German word *Verzweiflung* (despair), Pieper suggests here that the *zwei* (two) in this word reflects the divisive effect of despair on the human spirit [Tr.].

[10] II, II, 20, 3.

[11] Matthew, hom. 86, caput 4, col. 768, PG 58.

persistent, blasphemous resistance to grace, whereas he says of despair only that it is difficult for it to find forgiveness.[12] It is difficult for this reason: that despair, in that it "closes the door" (here again the picturesque Frankish idiom of Saint Paschasius Radbert[13]), is by its very nature a denial of the way that leads to the forgiveness of sin.

"In both good and bad, one proceeds, as a rule, from what is imperfect to what is perfect."[14] A sin as "perfect" as despair is normally not the first sin to be committed nor does it "just happen". Rather, the beginning and the root of despair is *acedia*, sloth.

There is hardly another concept that has become so demonstrably "at home" in the consciousness of the average Christian as that of *acedia*. (This fact is due in part to the usual translation of the word as Trägheit: "sloth",[15] which, while it coincides to some extent with the most immediate meaning of

[12] Mal., 3, 15.

[13] De fide, spe et charitate, liber II, caput VI, 2.

[14] II, II, 14, 4 ad 1.

[15] In this and the following paragraphs, Pieper is pointing out the difference of meaning between Greek *acedia* and its usual German translation *Trägheit*. Since German *Trägheit* is generally equivalent to English *sloth* (i.e., disinclination to labor), it has been possible to translate this passage as a contrast of meaning between the Greek and English terms without doing violence to Pieper's thought [Tr.].

the Greek word *akedia*, reflects only imperfectly and incompletely its true conceptual meaning.)

In popular thought the "capital sin" of sloth revolves around the proverb "An idle mind is the Devil's workshop". According to this concept, sloth is the opposite of diligence and industry; it is almost regarded as a synonym for laziness and idleness. Consequently, *acedia* has become, to all practical purposes, a concept of the middle class work ethic. The fact that it is numbered among the seven "capital sins" seems, as it were, to confer the sanction and approval of religion on the absence of leisure in the capitalistic industrial order.

But this is not just to render superficial and shallow the original concept of *acedia* as it exists in moral theology; it is to transform it completely.

According to the classical theology of the Church, *acedia* is a kind of sadness (*species tristitiae*[16])—more specifically, a sadness in view of the divine good in man. This sadness because of the God-given ennobling of human nature causes inactivity, depression, discouragement (thus the element of actual "sloth" is secondary).

The opposite of *acedia* is not industry and diligence, but magnanimity and that joy which is a fruit of the supernatural love of God. Not only can *acedia* and ordinary diligence exist very well to-

---

[16] I, II, 35, 8; II, II, 35; Mal., 11; Ver. 26, 4 ad 6.

gether; it is even true that the senselessly exaggerated workaholism of our age is directly traceable to *acedia*, which is a basic characteristic of the spiritual countenance of precisely this age in which we live. (The meaningless expression "Work and don't lose hope" offers some elucidation of this relationship.) The indolence expressed by the term *acedia* is so little the opposite of "work" in the ordinary meaning of the term that Saint Thomas says rather that *acedia* is a sin against the third of the Ten Commandments, by which man is enjoined to "rest his spirit in God".[17] Genuine rest and leisure (Muße) are possible only under the precondition that man accepts his own true meaning.

In the classical theology of the Church, *acedia* is understood to mean "*tristitia saeculi*",[18] that "sorrow according to the world" of which Paul says, in the Second Epistle to the Corinthians (7:10), that it "produces death".

This sorrow is a lack of magnanimity; it lacks courage for the great things that are proper to the nature of the Christian. It is a kind of anxious vertigo that befalls the human individual when he becomes aware of the height to which God has raised him. One who is trapped in *acedia* has

[17] II, II, 35, 3 ad 1; Mal., 11, 3 ad 2.
[18] Mal., 11, 3.

neither the courage nor the will to be as great as he really is. He would prefer to be less great in order thus to avoid the obligation of greatness. *Acedia* is a perverted humility; it will not accept supernatural goods because they are, by their very nature, linked to a claim on him who receives them. Something similar exists in the sphere of mental health and illness. The psychiatrist frequently observes that, while a neurotic individual may have a superficial will to be restored to health, in actuality he fears more than anything else the demands that are made, as a matter of course, on one who is well.

The more *acedia* advances from the region of emotion into that of intellectual decision, the more it becomes a deliberate turning away from, an actual fleeing from God. Man flees from God because God has exalted human nature to a higher, a divine, state of being and has thereby enjoined on man a higher standard of obligation. *Acedia* is, in the last analysis, a *detestatio boni divini*,[19] with the monstrous result that, upon reflection, man expressly wishes that God had not ennobled him, but had "left him in peace".[20]

As a capital sin, sloth is man's joyless, ill-tempered, and narrow-mindedly self-seeking re-

[19] Mal., 8, 1 ad 7.
[20] II, II, 35, 3.

jection of the nobility of the children of God with all the obligations it entails. As a genuine possibility and necessity, however, this "being a child of God" is an irrevocable fact that no one can alter. And since this irrevocable fact, which is not to be compared with the external offer of some gift or other, is precisely the renewal of man's whole nature at the center of his being, *acedia* means, in the last analysis, that man will not be what God wants him to be—in other words, that he will not be what he really is.

Acedia is what Kierkegaard, in his book on despair (*Sickness unto Death*), has called the "despair of weakness", which he considers a preliminary stage of despair proper and which consists in the fact that an individual "is unwilling, in his despair, to be himself".

Though not the only offspring of *acedia*, despair is the most legitimate. Saint Thomas Aquinas has assembled the *filiae acediae*, the companions and peers of despair, in a demonic constellation[21] that it will be rewarding to consider for a moment. For, since this association is not accidental, but is actually founded on their common origin, the knowledge of their relationship casts an illuminating light on the nature of despair.

[21] Mal., 11, 4; II, II, 35, 4 ad 2.

In addition to despair, *acedia* gives birth to that uneasy restlessness of mind that Thomas calls *evagatio mentis*: "No one can remain in sadness";[22] but since it is precisely his most inward being that causes the sadness of one who has fallen prey to *acedia*, the result is that such a one struggles to break out of the peace at the center of his own being.

For its part, *evagatio mentis* reveals itself in loquaciousness (*verbositas*), in excessive curiosity (*curiositas*), in an irreverent urge "to pour oneself out from the peak of the mind onto many things" (*importunitas*), in interior restlessness (*inquietudo*), and in instability of place or purpose (*instabilitas loci vel propositi*).[23] All these concepts that are inseparably related to "uneasy restlessness of mind" (*evagatio mentis*) are to be met with again in Heidegger's analysis of "everyday existence" (which, however, is not concerned with the religious significance of *acedia*): "being's flight from itself", "loquaciousness", "curiosity" as concern about the "possibility of abandoning oneself to the world", "importunity", "distraction", "instability".

Evagatio mentis and despair are followed by a third offspring of *acedia*—a sluggish indifference

[22] Mal., 11, 4.
[23] II, II, 35, 4 ad 3.

(*torpor*) toward those things that are in truth necessary for man's salvation; it is linked by an inner necessity to the denial of man's higher self that springs from sadness and sloth. The fourth offspring is pusillanimity (*pusillanimitas*) toward all the mystical opportunities that are open to man. The fifth is irritable rebellion (*rancor*) against all who are charged with the responsibility of preventing man's true and divinized self from falling prey to forgetfulness, to "self-forgetfulness". The last offspring is *malitia*, malice par excellence, a conscious inner choice and decision in favor of evil as evil that has its source in hatred for the divine in man.[24]

We have said that slothful sadness (*acedia*) is one of the determining characteristics of the hidden profile of our age, of an age that has proclaimed the standard of a "world of total work". This sloth, as the visible mark of secularization, determines the face of every age in which the call to tasks that are genuinely Christian begins to lose its official power to bind. *Acedia* is the signature of every age that seeks, in its despair, to shake off the obligations of that nobility of being that is conferred by Christianity and so, in its despair, to deny its true self.

[24] Mal., 3, 14 ad 8.

Is not the mere listing of the "offspring of sloth", of the siblings and peers of despair, a most striking confirmation of this diagnosis? Do we not read it with something approaching the shamefaced chagrin of a person who has been surprised in dishonest dealings? Does not the present era witness the ripening of all these fruits of despairing sadness?

These things are not said here for the sake of the easy and all too cheap pleasure of pointing out the weaknesses of our age. Moreover, temptations to *acedia* and despair are not temptations that lose their power if one averts one's eyes from them. Temptations to *acedia* and despair can be overcome only by the vigilant resistance of an alert and steady watchfulness.[25] Despair (except, perhaps, one's awareness of it) is not destroyed by "work", but only by that clear-sighted magnanimity that courageously expects and has confidence in the greatness of its own nature and by the grace-filled impetus of the hope of eternal life.

The root and origin of despair is the slothful sadness of *acedia*. But its "perfection" is accompanied by pride. Theology has pointed out often enough the relationship between pride and despair. When an individual whose despair springs initially "from

[25] II, II, 35, 1 ad 4.

weakness" comes "to realize why he does not want to be himself, then it changes suddenly, and defiance steps in" (Kierkegaard).

Pride is the hidden conduit that links the two diametrically opposed forms of hopelessness, despair and presumption. At the nadir of despair, the self-destructive and perverse rejection of fulfillment borders on the most extreme form of the not less destructive delusion of presumption—the affirmation of nonfulfillment as though it were fulfillment.

Chapter Four

ANTICIPATION OF FULFILLMENT
(PRESUMPTION)

By implanting in man the new "future" of a practically inexhaustible "not yet", supernatural hope lays the foundation for a new youthfulness that can be destroyed only if hope is destroyed. In both forms of hopelessness—in despair as well as in presumption—the youthfulness of one who hopes is reduced, as it were, to nothingness, but in different ways: in the case of despair, by senility; in presumption, by infantility.

The "infantility" of presumption lies in its perverse anticipation of fulfillment. Because man comes to believe that he has actually attained the "arduous" goal that, in reality, lies still in the future, the tension of hope is relaxed in the middle of the "way" and passes into the peaceful certainty of possession.

The (objectively speaking) "inopportune" character of presumption has in it a certain element of comedy, whereas despair has rather an element of tragedy.

Incidentally, presumption is less opposed to hope than is despair. For despair is the true antitype of hope, whereas presumption is but its *falsa similitudo*,[1] its fraudulent imitation. In much the same way, infantility has a false and merely "imitative" resemblance to true youthfulness, the proper antitype of which is aging.

[1] II, II, 21, 3.

The presumption that is opposed to the theological virtue of hope is the individual's perverted attitude toward the fact that eternal life is the meaning and goal of our earthly "way".

We are not speaking, then, of that other presumption that has to do with natural powers and goals. More than a hundred questions will intervene in the *Summa* before Thomas will devote two articles to this kind of presumption.[2]

The presumption of which we speak is, rather, an attitude of mind that fails to accept the reality of the futurity and "arduousness" that characterize eternal life. In conjunction with attainability, these two characteristics—futurity and "arduousness"—constitute the formal nature of the object of hope.[3] If one of these characteristics is missing or ceases to be genuine, hope is no longer possible. In other words, presumption destroys supernatural hope by failing to recognize it for what it is; by not acknowledging that earthly existence in the *status viatoris* is, in a precise and proper sense, the "way" to ultimate fulfillment, and by regarding eternal life as something that is "basically" already achieved, as something that is "in principle" already given.

The notion of overconfidence, of an overreaching

[2] II, II, 130.
[3] I, II, 40, 1.

of oneself,[4] that is never absent from the false anticipation that is presumption clearly indicates the negative relationship of presumption to reality.

For the essential nature of presumption is, as Saint Augustine says, a *"perversa securitas"*,[5] a self-deceptive reliance on a security that has no existence in reality. In the last analysis, what appears to be a "superhuman" element in the anticipation of fulfillment is, in reality, none other than a yielding to the, if not exactly "heroic", yet certainly not despicable, weight of man's need for security. In the sin of presumption, man's desire for security is so exaggerated that it exceeds the bounds of reality. It is important to keep in mind what presumption really is.

Presumption reveals itself in two basic forms that correspond to the mutually opposed pretexts on which it bases its inordinate satisfaction.[6]

Theology calls the first kind of presumption "Pelagian". It is characterized by the more or less explicit thesis that man is able by his own human

[4] Pieper uses here the German words *ver-messenheit* and *sich ver-messen* (cf. note in Chap. 3), hyphenating them in order to give full weight to the prefix (*"ver-"*), which in German often signals a reversal or distortion of meaning [Tr.].

[5] Sermo 87, 8, col. 535, PL 38.

[6] II, II, 21, 4.

nature to win eternal life and the forgiveness of sins. Associated with it is the typically liberal, bourgeois moralism that, for no apparent reason, is antagonistic not only to dogma per se, but also to the sacramental reality of the Church: solely on the basis of his own moral "performance", an "upright" and "decent" individual who "does his duty" will be able to "stand the test before God" as well.

Between this first basic kind of presumption and the second lies that pseudo-religious activism that believes it can construct, out of a thousand "exercises", a claim to the kingdom of heaven that is rightful and absolutely valid and able, as it were, to pit itself against God. The frantically self-assured features of infantilism are especially visible here.

The second form of presumption, in which, admittedly, its basic character as a kind of premature certainty is obscured, has its roots in the heresy propagated by the Reformation, viz., the sole efficacy of God's redemptive and engracing action. By teaching the absolute certainty of salvation solely by virtue of the merits of Christ, this heresy destroys the true pilgrim character of Christian existence by making as certain for the individual Christian as the revealed fact of redemption the belief that he had already "actually" achieved the goal of salvation. (Moreover, the theology of the Reformation thereby of necessity denied not only the negativity of the "not yet", but also its positive side: in no sense does it regard man's proper existence as a positive progression toward fulfillment.) It has often been observed how close—both logically and psychologically—this second form of presumption is to despair on the one hand and, on the other, to the moral uninhibitedness of that "inordinate trust in God's mercy" that theology reckons, along with despair, among the "sins against the Holy Spirit". It is but proper to emphasize at this point what is surely obvious: that we are speaking here only of the objective erroneousness of the presumption that is part of Reformation theology. It would be ridiculous and absurd to raise or attempt to answer the question of subjective guilt.

Presumption has its source in a self-esteem that, while false, is somehow affirmed by the individual's own will; it consists in the will to achieve a certainty that is necessarily invalid because there is no valid ground for it. Even more specifically, this false esteem of oneself is a lack of humility, a denial of one's actual creatureliness, and an unnatural claim to being like God.[7] Hope presupposes

[7] II, II, 21, 4; Mal., 8, 2.

not only magnanimity, but also humility. Saint Augustine says in his *Commentary on the Psalms* that only to the humble is it given to hope.[8]

Despair and presumption block the approach to true prayer. For prayer, in its original form as a prayer of petition, is nothing other than the voicing of hope.

One who despairs does not petition because he assumes that his prayer will not be granted. One who is presumptuous petitions, indeed, but his petition is not genuine because he fully anticipates its fulfillment.

This sheds a new light on the words of Holy Scripture: "that they [the Lord's disciples] must always pray and not lose heart" (Lk 18:1). Explicit in these words is the never-ceasing necessity of a hope that is humble enough really to pray and, at the same time, magnanimous enough to wait cooperatively for the fulfillment of its prayer.

In theological hope the "antithesis" between divine justice and divine mercy is, as it were, "removed"—not so much "theoretically", as existentially: supernatural hope is man's appropriate, existential answer to the fact that these qualities in God, which to the creature appear to be

[8] Psalm 118, 15, 2, col. 1541, PL 37.

ANTICIPATION OF FULFILLMENT

contradictory, are actually identical. One who looks only at the justice of God is as little able to hope as is one who sees only the mercy of God. Both fall prey to hopelessness—one to the hopelessness of despair, the other to the hopelessness of presumption. Only hope is able to comprehend the reality of God that surpasses all antitheses, to know that his mercy is identical with his justice and his justice with his mercy.

Presumption, however, is the lesser, and despair the greater, sin: "Because of his infinite goodness, it is more proper to God to spare and to show mercy than to punish. For the former belongs to him by reason of his nature, the latter only by reason of our sins".[9] In other words, the anticipation of fulfillment is not so contrary to man's real existential situation as is the anticipation of nonfulfillment. The ungrounded certainty of presumption is less contrary to human nature than is despair.

Nevertheless, it remains true that presumption is a sin in the real and strict sense; in its most extreme form, it is, indeed, a sin against the Holy Spirit.

That ultimate existential uncertainty, the root of which—so long as we remain in the *status viatoris*—is the ever-present possibility of volun-

[9] II, II, 21, 2.

tary defection, is inevitably present even in the lives of the saints. It is inseparable from the concept of being on the way. It is wholly impossible for "pilgrim man"—and hence cannot constitute a valid goal for him—to escape from this uncertainty into absolute certainty. Absolute certainty is unattainable, even "in principle", for *homo viator*. What this realization amounts to is this: in the existential uncertainty that is his natural lot, man understands himself as a finite nature that does not have being from himself and therefore does not possess himself—that is, as a creature—and that takes refuge in the merciful power of God's decrees.

The uncertainty of human existence cannot be totally removed. But it can be "overcome"—by hope, and only by hope.

The precariousness of the "potentiality for being" that is a mark of creaturely existence is reflected in the fact that hope lives intimately with fear. This union of hope and fear is operative not only in the natural sphere, but also—a concept that is full of mystery and difficult to comprehend—in the supernatural sphere. Theological hope is essentially linked to the fear that is counted among the seven gifts of the Holy Spirit: the "fear of the Lord".[10]

[10] II, II, 19, 9 ad 1.

It is this fear that is excluded by the false certainty of presumptive anticipation.[11] And because presumption shuts out fear, it also shuts out the virtue of hope, which is based on the fact that fulfillment has "not yet" been accomplished and that nonfulfillment has "not yet" been excluded.

[11] II, II, 21, 3 ad 3.

Chapter Five

THE GIFT OF FEAR

ONE OF THE LAST VERIFIABLE of the theses that define the image of man for our time holds that it is not seemly for man to be afraid.

Waters from two sources are mingled in this attitude. One is an enlightened liberalism that relegates fearfulness to the realm of the unreal and in whose world view, accordingly, there is no room for fear except in the figurative sense. The other is an un-Christian stoicism that is secretly allied with both presumption and despair and confronts in defiant invulnerability—without fear, but also without hope—the evils of existence, which it sees with admirable clarity.

The classical theology of the Church is equally removed from both the oversimplification of liberalism and the desperate rigidity of stoicism. It takes for granted that fears are a reality of human existence. And it takes equally for granted that man will respond to what is objectively fearful with fear.

However, the real concern of classical theology is with something quite different; hence it regards fear from a very different point of view. It inquires into the *ordo timoris*,[1] into the due order of fear—that is, into the various (negative) gradations of the objects of fear. It praises or blames not fear itself,

[1] II, II, 125, 1 ad 1.

but the order or lack of order that is manifest in it. "Fear embodies the concept of sin in so far as it is opposed to the order of reason",[2] that is, insofar as it is opposed to the objective truth of reality. This is true, however, not only of fear, but also of fearlessness. Among the sins opposed to the virtue of fortitude (and one cannot say this too emphatically: the virtue of fortitude!), Saint Thomas lists not only disordered fear, but also unnatural fearlessness (*intimiditas*).[3]

In its concept of man, classical theology is aware of a fearlessness that bespeaks a lack of fortitude as well as of a fearfulness that is not only not "unworthy", but actually ethical; that accords with the nature of reality and with the spiritual dignity of man. (I have tried to show elsewhere[4] how little the possibility of genuine fortitude is involved here.) On the basis of this theology one must assume, then, that something is not quite in order when a man is afraid of nothing, and that the ideal of "stoic" invulnerability and fearlessness is based on a false interpretation of man and of reality itself.

Thomas Aquinas points, in particular, to three passages of Holy Scripture, which, incidentally, are scarcely known to contemporary Christianity,

[2] II, II, 125, 4.
[3] II, II, 126.
[4] Fortitude (Eng. trans.), pp. 24–33.

as proof that fearlessness as a fundamental attitude—which, in any event, can "be maintained" only through self-deception—is nothing short of unnatural. According to Thomas,[5] the first passage, which is from the book of Job, refers to fearlessness that has its source in a presumptuous pride of mind: ". . . He was made to fear no one" (Job 41:24); the second passage[6] is from Sirach: ". . . He that is without fear cannot be justified . . ." (Sir 1:28); the third is from the book of Proverbs: "A wise man feareth and declineth from evil" (Prov 14:16).[7]

In the present context, however, we are speaking of fear only "insofar as it somehow turns us to God",[8] that is, we are speaking of the "fear of the Lord". This is true also of what follows. If we consider the matter from a metaphysical rather than a psychological point of view, this fear is that "partial truth"—often so disguised as to be unrecognizable—that lies hidden in all the other fears and anxieties that plague mankind.

It is not easy for contemporary man to come to an understanding of what is really meant by the classical concept of "fear of the Lord" and "fear of

[5] II, II, 126, 1.
[6] II, II, 126, 1 ad 1.
[7] II, II, 126, 1 ad 2.
[8] II, II, 19, 2.

God": too many liberal and stoic obstructions stand in the way.

From the beginning, one must keep firmly in mind that fear of the Lord is, in the undiminished and precise sense of the word, truly "fear". Fear of the Lord is not the same as "respect" for God. This popular misunderstanding and attenuation robs the concept of most of its original meaning. It is just as inexact—and opens the way to a similar misunderstanding—to interpret it as "reverence" or "awe". The fact that classical theology expressly teaches that fear of the Lord—although wholly directed to God—still is obviously not a fear "of" God, in the sense in which one might speak of the fear "of" some misfortune, is one indication among others of how far these euphemisms fall short of the true meaning of "fear of the Lord".[9] Such a distinction would be totally meaningless if fear of the Lord were understood as "reverence" or "respect"; for, formally speaking, acts of reverence and respect are referred to God in the same direct sense in which fear is directed to evil.

It remains, then, to inquire what it is that fear of the Lord fears.

It has become customary in our age to speak—and

[9] II, II, 19, 1.

not always without self-complacency—of man's imperiled and threatened existence. But the words are seldom used to refer to the utmost and ultimate danger which threatens man's existence and before which every other threat of catastrophe and destruction, even on a planetary scale, and every other danger inherent in the struggle for existence are secondary and even unreal. This ultimate threat, which introduces into the very core of human existence the real possibility of a diminution and corruption of being, is none other than the *posse peccare*, the ability to commit sin. This statement must, of course, be freed from its exclusive moralistic connotation and linked once more to its original and deeper meaning—its reference to being itself.

It is to the fearfulness of this very real possibility, which is always rising anew from the ground of the creature's being—to the fearfulness of being separated by sin from the Ultimate Ground of all being—that the fear of the Lord, which is a true fearfulness, affords the only true answer.

No "heroism" can overcome this fear. Its object is inseparably and irrevocably linked to the nature of "pilgrim man's" existence. One can, perhaps, turn one's gaze from what gives rise to this fear; one can, perhaps and as it were, forget the fear of the Lord. But to do so is to forget oneself, to contradict the reality of one's own existence.

There are two ways of fearing the possibility of incurring sin: because of the sin itself or because of the punishment due it. The more genuine fear is the fear of sin as sin. But because punishment is not linked to sin by an "arbitrary ruling" of God and, as it were, *ex post facto*, but is directly linked to and proceeds from the very nature of sin, it follows that a fear that is initially linked to punishment can nevertheless be, in a genuine sense, a fear of sin.

Theology calls this true fear of sin a *timor filialis* or a *timor castus*, a "filial" or "chaste" fear. (The latter designation originated with the Fathers of the Church and is no longer wholly comprehensible to us today.) The other kind of fear is called *timor servilis*, a "servile" fear.

"Servile" fear is an imperfect fear of the Lord. It has its source—"All fear is born of love";[10] fear is "love in flight"[11]—in an imperfect form of "concupiscent" love of God. The *timor servilis* fears above all the loss of personal fulfillment in eternal life—in other words, eternal damnation. Therein lies the nature and substance of "servile" fear.[12]

Although it is something imperfect, this substance of "servile" fear, namely the fear of eternal

[10] II, II, 126, 1.
[11] De civitate Dei, liber 14, caput 7, col. 410, PL 41.
[12] II, II, 19, 4 ad 3.

punishment, is nevertheless "good";[13] indeed, it is "from the Holy Spirit".[14] It can pave the way for a true love of God (*caritas*);[15] and it is the "beginning of wisdom" (Ps 111:10), for it disposes the soul for wisdom.[16] Today, we can hardly bring ourselves to reflect on these teachings. There are many reasons for this. In addition to the general inhibitions that have their source in liberalism and stoicism, which we have mentioned above, there is also a more specific reason: above all, that the "last things"—heaven and hell—have come to be, in the public consciousness and even among Christians, something not to be taken seriously. Heaven has been reduced to a playground and the angels to playmates of small children, whereas for Saint Thomas Aquinas the apparition of an angel had the character of something elementally frightening and confusing—which explained why an angel's first word to man was always "Be not afraid."[17] In like manner, hell and the fallen angels have become less real to us because they have been stripped of their natural state as spiritual realities and thus of their ultimate awesomeness.

As a reason for turning to God, fear of eternal

[13] II, II, 19, 4.
[14] II, II, 19, 9.
[15] II, II, 19, 8 ad 1.
[16] II, II, 19, 7.
[17] III, 30, 3 ad 3.

damnation belongs admittedly to an imperfect level of love of God. Yet, on this level of the interior life, it is the only possibility of an appropriate existential answer to one of the most central realities of human existence. It is impossible—again, at this level of love—to "overcome" one's anxiety in the face of eternal punishment; neither "a proper attitude" nor indifference nor optimism is sufficient for this purpose. In any event, even if it were possible, such a conquest could occur only in open conflict with the objective reality of being. The only victory over the fear of eternal damnation that is both genuine and appropriate to man's nature is advancement in love.

By that genuine love of God that affirms the Highest Good for its own sake, "servile" fear is transformed and raised to a fear that is both "filial" and "chaste".

It must be repeated here: "filial" fear is also genuine fear. In a certain sense, in fact, it incorporates the concept of fear more truly than does "servile" fear. For "filial" fear sees sin as sin; but sin is "evil" to a greater degree than punishment is.[18] Thus the fear of sin responds to a deeper imperilment of human existence than does the fear of eternal damnation. It has its dwelling closer to the innermost and most crucial core of man's intel-

[18] Mal., 1, 5.

lectual and moral existence, whereas fear of eternal punishment seems to be ordered rather to the psychic and emotional spheres. The "servile" fear of damnation decreases as man's nature is the more deeply penetrated by his love of friendship with God,[19] that is, the more closely he is bound to the eternal ground of his being. Because it is true fear, "filial" fear, on the other hand, increases as the love of God grows in intensity. This fact may, at first glance, seem surprising, but its inner necessity is revealed as one's understanding penetrates more deeply. On the one hand, the very real possibility of sin is not excluded for "pilgrim man" even on the highest level of the love of God; a voluntary defection from God is always "wholly possible" (*omnino possibilis*)[20] for him as long as he has "not yet" attained the *status comprehensoris*. On the other hand, the orientation toward nothingness and the reduction to nothingness that is the true nature of sin is evident only to one who is a "friend of God"; only supernatural love of God—fear is "love in flight"—at once enables and compels the individual to fear the possibility of sin as greatly as its very genuine fearfulness demands.

In a different sense than the "servile" fear of eternal damnation, the "chaste" fear of a sinful turning

[19] II, II, 19, 10.
[20] II, II, 19, 11.

away from God is also the "beginning of wisdom": the former prepares the soul for wisdom; the latter is the first fruit of wisdom itself.[21]

"Filial" fear, which is ordered to the perfect love of God, is numbered among the gifts of the Holy Spirit. It is a gift that entirely surpasses the potentialities of natural man.[22]

Ethical good is none other than the development and perfection of the natural tendencies of our nature:[23] it is man's natural fear of the diminution and annihilation of his being; its perfection lies in the fear of the Lord.

From this statement we may draw some noteworthy conclusions. If man's natural anxiety in the face of nothingness is not perfected by the fear of the Lord, it erupts "unperfected" and destructive into the realm of his intellectual and spiritual existence. The dominance of this "unperfected", destructive anxiety is a sign that an individual has voluntarily denied and rejected the fear of the Lord. The fear of the Lord, however, is characteristic of and intrinsic to every good human act; by the same token, it is somehow excluded and lost through every sin.[24] Hence "unperfected"

[21] II, II, 19, 7.
[22] II, II, 19, 9.
[23] II, II, 108, 2.
[24] Mal., 8, 2 ad 5.

THE GIFT OF FEAR

anxiety is the mark and accompaniment of (objective) sin, that is, of what is contrary to reality. At this point, theology is once again in accord with the findings of modern psychiatry.

There is only one possible way in which man's natural anxiety in the face of nothingness can penetrate his intellectual and psychic life *without* immediately destroying it. This one way is the perfecting of natural anxiety by the fear of the Lord. Only the fear of the Lord contains in itself the ontological ground of all "health": it accords with reality.

Fear of the Lord and the theological virtue of hope are naturally ordered to one another; they complement one another.[25] Our hesitation in acknowledging this complementarity seems to find its counterpart and confirmation in the fact that even Saint Thomas, who changed his opinion in only a few recorded instances, stated this relationship of hope and fear of the Lord clearly and definitively only in the second part of the second major part of the *Summa*—something he had not done in the first part or in his earlier commentary on the *Sentences* of Peter Lombard.

The link between hope and fear is that "concupiscent" love that seeks God first for its own sake. This love, as we have seen, is the foundation

[25] II, II, 141, 1 ad 3.

of hope, and fear is its "negative side". We can hope and fear only for ourselves (and for those we love).

"Servile" fear corresponds to that level of hope that has not yet been molded by *caritas*, by the true love of friendship for God. "Chaste" or "filial" fear is the "negative side" of the loving hope that is contained in the love of friendship.

Fear of the Lord assures the genuineness of hope. It eliminates the danger that hope may be turned into its *falsa similitudo*, its false image: into the presumptuous anticipation of fulfillment. Fear of the Lord keeps ever before the mind of one who hopes the fact that fulfillment has "not yet" been accomplished. Fear of the Lord is the constant reminder that human existence, although destined for and oriented toward fulfillment by the Highest Being, is, nevertheless, perpetually threatened in the *status viatoris* by the closeness of nothingness.

Paschasius Radbert comments with an appositeness we can but admire: "Holy fear guards the summit of hope."[26]

In Holy Scripture (Ps 115:11), the same thought is expressed in language that is at once simple and elegant: "They who fear the Lord trust in the Lord."

[26] De fide, spe et charitate, liber II, caput VII, 1.

AUTHOR'S REMARKS

For the thoughts expressed in this book, I am indebted above all to the study of the works of Saint Thomas Aquinas.

Of the monographs available to me, first mention must be made of the excellent *Commentary on the Six Questions on Hope* (II, II, 17–22) by the Dominican, J. Le Tilly, in the French edition of the *Summa Theologica* (Paris: *Editions de la Revue des Jeunes*, 1929).

The numerous references to the texts of Saint Thomas Aquinas, especially to the *Summa Theologica* and the *Quaestiones Disputatae*, are not intended to be "historical". No attempt has been made to reconstruct in historical form the world of ideas of the "greatest systematic theologian of the high Middle Ages". What has been attempted is, rather, the building of a bridge to the work of the "universal teacher" of the Church inasmuch as it shares in the present magisterium of the Church itself, which is above history.

Only the numerical references have been given for the frequent quotations from the *Summa Theologica*. The designation "II, II, 19, 9 ad 1", for example, means *Summa Theologica*, Second Part of the Second Part, Question 19, Article 9, answer to the First Objection. The same procedure has been followed for Thomas's *Commentary on the Sentences of Peter Lombard*, although the numerical pattern is different. The designation "3, d. 26, 1, 5", for example, means *Commentum in IV Libros Sententiarum*, Book 3, Distinction 26, Question 1, Article 5.

Note: Pieper concludes his remarks by listing, with their customary abbreviations, the titles of other works of Saint Thomas Aquinas that are cited in the text. I have incorporated this listing into the bibliographical information given in the following Translator's Note. [Tr.]

TRANSLATOR'S NOTE

Full bibliographical information for all works cited in the text is as follows:

Basic Texts

St. Thomas Aquinas, *Summa Theologiae*, 60 vols. (New York: McGraw Hill, 1964–1975). Note: The numerical references in this edition of the *Summa Theologiae*, which contains the text in both Latin and English, are in a slightly different form from that described above in the Author's Remarks (e.g., for II, II, 19, read 2a, 2ae, 19).

St. Thomas Aquinas, "Commentum in Librum II Sententiarum", in *Opera Omnia*, vol. VIII (Paris: apud Ludovicum Vivès, 1873).

St. Thomas Aquinas, *Quaestiones Disputatae*, 2 vols. (Rome: Marietti, 1949). Individual *Quaestiones* are listed below under Other Works Cited.

Patrologiae Cursus Completus, series latina, J. P. Migne, ed., 221 vols. (Paris: 1857–1866). Cited as PL.

Patrologiae Cursus Completus, series graeca, J. P. Migne, ed., 161 vols. (Paris: 1857–1866). Cited as PG.

Other Works Cited
(in order of appearance with customary abbreviations)

Mal.	*Quaestiones Disputatae de Malo*.
De pec.	St. Augustine, "De peccatorum meritis et remissione, et de baptismo parvulorum . . . libri tres", PL 44, cols. 109–200. (For an English translation, see "On the Merits and Remission of Sins, and on the Baptism of Infants" in *A Select Library of the Nicene and*

	Post-Nicene Fathers of the Christian Church, Series I, vol. V, ed. Philip Schaff [New York: Charles Scribner's Sons, 1908], pp. 11–78.)
Quol.	St. Thomas Aquinas, *Quaestiones Quodlibetales* (Rome: Marietti, 1949).
Pot.	*Questiones Disputatae de Potentia Dei.* (For an English translation, see St. Thomas Aquinas, *On the Power of God* [Three Books in One], trans. English Dominican Fathers [Westminster, Md.: Newman, 1952].)
Virt. card.	*Quaestio Disputata de Virtutibus Cardinalibus.*
Virt. comm.	*Quaestio Disputata de Virtutibus in Communi.* (For an English translation, see St. Thomas Aquinas, *The Virtues [in General]*, trans. John Patrick Reid, O.P. [Providence: Providence College Press, 1951].)
Contra Graecos	St. Thomas Aquinas, "Declaratio Quorumdam Articulorum Contra Graecos, Armenos et Saracenos" in *Opuscula Selecta*, vol. I (Paris: Lethielleux, 1881), pp. 220–246.
Cajetan	St. Thomas Aquinas, *Secunda Secundae Partis Summae Totius Theologiae*, Reverendissimi Domini Thomae a Vio (Cajetan), . . . illustrata (Lyons: apud Ioannam Iacobi Iuntae F., 1581).
De spe	*Quaestio Disputata de Spe.*

Council of Trent	*Concilium Tridentinum: Diariorum, Actorum, Epistularum, Tractatuum*, Nova Collectio, vol. 5, ed. Stephanus Ehses (Freiburg: Herder, 1911).
St. Bonaventure	St. Bonaventure, "Commentaria in IV Libros Sententiarum Magistri Petri Lombardi" in *Opera Theologica Selecta*, 4 vols., . . . Cura PP. Collegii S. Bonaventurae edita (Florence: Ad claras aquas, 1934–1949).
De fide, spe et charitate	St. Paschasius Radbert, "De fide, spe et charitate" in *Opera Omnia*, PL 120, cols. 1387–1490.
Hebr.	St. Thomas Aquinas, "In Epistolam ad Hebraeos", *Opera Omnia*, vol. 21 (Paris: apud Ludovicus Vivès, 1876), pp. 561–734.
Contra Faustum	St. Augustine, "Contra Faustum Manichaeum Libri XXXIII", PL 42. (For an English translation, see St. Augustine, "Reply to Faustus the Manichaean", in *A Select Library of the Nicene and Post-Nicene Fathers of the Christian Church;* Series I, vol. IV, ed. Philip Schaff [New York: Charles Scribner's Sons, 1909], pp. 151–345.)
Sermo	St. Augustine, "Sermones Classes Quatuor" in *Opera Omnia*, PL 38.
Comp.	St. Thomas Aquinas, "Compendium Theologiae", in *Opuscula Selecta*, vol. I (Paris: Lethielleux, 1881), pp. 1–219.

	(For an English translation, see St. Thomas Aquinas, *Compendium of Theology*, trans. Cyril Vollert, S.J., S.T.D. [London: Herder, 1947].)
Paradise	Dante Alighieri, *The Divine Comedy*, part III: *Paradise*, trans. Dorothy L. Sayers and Barbara Reynolds (Baltimore: Penguin Books, 1962).
De genesi	St. Augustine, "De Genesi ad Litteram Libri XII" in *Opera Omnia*, PL 34, cols. 245–486. (For an English translation, see St. Augustine, *The Literal Meaning of Genesis*, 2 vols., trans. John Hammond Taylor, S.J., in *Ancient Christian Writers*, vols. 41–42 [New York: Newman, 1982].)
Isidore	St. Isidore, "Sententiarum Libri Tres", in PL 83, cols. 537–738.
De Isaac	St. Ambrose, "De Isaac et Anima Liber Unus", PL 14, cols. 523–560. (For an English translation, see St. Ambrose, "Isaac, or the Soul", *Seven Exegetical Works*, in *The Fathers of the Church*, vol. 65 [Washington: Catholic University Press, 1972], pp. 9–65.)
Matthew	St. John Chrysostom, "Homiliarum in Matthaeum Continuatio", PG 58. (For an English translation, see "The Homilies of St. John Chrysostom . . . on the Gospel of St. Matthew", trans. Rev. Sir George Prevost, in *A Select Library of the Nicene and Post-Nicene*

	Fathers of the Christian Church, Series I, ed. Philip Schaff [New York: Charles Scribner's Sons, 1908].)
Ver.	*Quaestiones Disputatae de Veritate.* (For an English translation, see St. Thomas Aquinas, *Truth*, trans. Robert W. Mulligan, S.J., 3 vols. [Chicago: Regnery Press, 1952–1954].)
Psalm	St. Augustine, "Enarrationes in Psalmos", PL 36–37.
Fortitude	Pieper quotes from the third edition of his book *Vom Sinn der Tapferkeit* (pp. 53 ff.), which I have been unable to locate. For an English translation of the text, the reader is referred, however, to Josef Pieper, *Fortitude and Temperance*, trans. Daniel F. Coogan (New York: Pantheon, 1954), which contains the translation of two books by Pieper: *Vom Sinn der Tapferkeit* and *Zucht und Mass*.
De civitate Dei	St. Augustine, *De civitate Dei,* libri XXII, in PL 41. (For an English translation, see St. Augustine, *The City of God*, 3 vols. in *The Fathers of the Church* [New York: The Fathers of the Church, vols. 8 (1950), 14 (1952), 24 (1954)].)